Elizabeth Volk Long,
publisher,
Time
"Good sense and great fun. A quick and entertaining read, it's bound to be a winner."

Victor Doolan,
president,
BMW of North America
"It is amazing how in two hours one can acquire more business wisdom than can be acquired from a lifetime of work. Many thanks for sharing this invaluable information with me."

Leonard Riggio,
president,
Barnes & Noble, Inc.
"A business book that takes more than two hours to read isn't worth the paper it's printed on. . . . Let's hope this book hits the charts as a business-book bestseller."

John Mack Carter,
editor in chief and director of
magazine development,
Good Housekeeping
"I can think of only one secret for success to add to this collection of 500 business maxims: Read this book."

Jack Kliger,
publisher,
Glamour
"The person who said you can't mix serious business with a good laugh has not read this book . . . and really needs to. As for myself, I need to get another copy. A friend was preparing to make a speech and, after reading the copy I had, literally stole it from me."

Ernst L. Wynder, M.D.,
president,
American Health Foundation
"A superb book."

Why Climb
the Corporate Ladder
When You Can Take
the Elevator?

———————— ♦ ————————

500 Secrets for Success
in Business

John M. Capozzi

JMC Industries, Inc.
125 Brett Lane
Fairfield, CT 06430
1997

Library of Congress Cataloging-in-Publication Data

Capozzi, John M.
Why climb the corporate ladder when you can take the elevator?
500 secrets for success in business / John M. Capozzi—1st ed.
p.   cm.
ISBN 0-9656410-1-5
1. Career development.   2. Career development—Quotations,
maxims, etc.   3. Management—Quotations, maxims, etc.
I. Title.

9 8 7 6 5 4 3 2
First Edition

This book is dedicated
to businesspeople everywhere
. . . may they enjoy what they are doing,
learn to do it better,
and prosper from doing it well.

INTRODUCTION

I had to work full-time to put myself through college. When I graduated in the 1960s, I was mentally and physically exhausted from my demanding schedule. In order to pay for my education, I worked Fridays, Saturdays, Sundays, and Mondays. I went to school from nine in the morning to ten at night Tuesday through Thursday for almost five years. It was like running a marathon interrupted every five miles with a hundred-yard dash just to make sure I didn't get too relaxed. During these years I held all sorts of jobs. While many of the things I learned in the classroom have faded with time, maxims I learned doing these jobs have provided me with experiences, skills, and insights that I am still using almost thirty years later.

One of my first college jobs was as a locker boy in an affluent men's health club directly across the street from the college. Members identified themselves at my window and I retrieved a small wire basket with their sneakers and gym clothing. There were several other college students who worked this job between classes. It was a great job that allowed us to get paid for doing homework when the work was slow.

One day a customer came to play squash, but his partner didn't show. He asked me if I would "hit" with him so that his court time wasn't a total loss. Having grown up in the New York area, my athletic skills at that moment consisted of knowing how to play stickball, how to fight, and how to run from all sorts of people. Squash was not in my repertoire. But, since I've never been one to turn down an offer without at least exploring it a little bit, I decided to hit with him. I just imagined that the racquet was a stickball bat that was very wide at the end. After about ten minutes I had learned to hit the ball well enough to give my partner a decent workout. I also discovered something else. I liked squash. I began to practice every day in between my locker duties and breaks from homework.

After a few weeks I was able to play reasonably

well. The word got around and members began to call on a frequent basis to book games with me when their regular squash partners weren't available. I became the de-facto club pro. The club loved it. It gave them another member service at no additional cost.

A few of my new squash friends held reasonably senior positions on Wall Street. One day one of them came in and during our game asked if I had any money to invest. I had about $500 . . . my life savings. He recommended a stock that I should buy "today." I thought about it and decided, "What the hell." I bought five hundred shares at a dollar a share in a company that, to this day, I haven't the foggiest notion of what they do. The hardest part of the transaction was finding a broker and opening an account. Credit history? None. Liabilities? Numerous. Assets? Zero. Employment? Locker boy and free-lance stock speculator with a net worth in the mid three figures.

But one of the wonderful things about America is that you can always find somebody to take your money if you've got some. Three days later my "new" company was bought by a larger company and I sold my five hundred shares for $1,500. This was more money than I had ever accumulated at one time in my entire life. From this venture I learned that, if you're a success with people, you can be successful in business.

During the winters of my college years, I'd leave New York late on Thursday nights and drive to Vermont where I worked from Friday to Monday as part of the ski patrol at Bromley Mountain. I loved this job. I'd get up at 5:00 A.M. every day and ride the snowcat up the mountain long before the lifts opened. I'd learned to ski during high school. I didn't ski with tremendous style, but I was strong and rarely fell. Good qualifications for any member of a ski patrol. I was driven to become a better skier, so I skied constantly. I was usually the first on the mountain and almost always the last off. I skied when it was ten below. I skied in the rain. By the time I graduated from college in 1965, I had become a good skier.

After college I decided to take some time off before launching myself into a career. I moved to Vermont and took a full-time job at Bromley Mountain. By now I skied well enough to race and I eventually became a professional ski instructor.

On Easter Sunday morning, I was involved in making a ski film. While doing a Royal Christie (skiing on only one ski with the other raised behind me so that it rested on my shoulder), I fell. The ski didn't release, but my leg did. I broke the tibia. While the cast was being put on, I gave a lot of thought to my immediate future as a ski instructor and determined that it was time to move on.

Monday morning, I did one of the dumbest things I had done to that date in my life. I sent a telegram to the head of personnel at American Airlines at La Guardia Airport. The telegram told him who I was, provided a minimal amount of personal background, and I stated that I was now ready for American Airlines to hire me. I was so naive that I wasn't even aware of how presumptuous I was being. It just seemed like the thing to do at the time.

As it turned out, this guy had never received such an unusual request for employment. Out of sheer curiosity, he replied with a telegram asking me to come in at 9:00 A.M. the following Tuesday for an interview.

On Tuesday I arrived at La Guardia about an hour early. As luck would have it, I walked into the building from the parking lot with the man I was to meet. Of course I didn't recognize him, even as he held the door open for me, crutches and all. I asked him if he knew where I might find Personnel. He did.

Under the circumstances, the interview went

very well. It turned out that the personnel manager was an avid skier and we got on like old friends. He offered me a position as a management understudy. Management understudy was a trainee position where you could expect to be promoted to supervisor in three years. I accepted and two weeks later started class to become a ticket agent at La Guardia.

My supervisor was a tough customer. He took no lip from anybody. He called me into his office on the first day of training. It was a small office and had no decorations of any kind except for a framed slogan on the wall behind his desk. That slogan read: "If you hide your light under a bushel, you can't be seen from above." He gave me the once-over and glanced at my very slim personnel file. Then he asked why I thought I should be his understudy. I glanced at the slogan behind him and told him it was because I was far and away the best candidate for the job. He thought about that for a moment and then went on with the interview.

As he outlined the management understudy position, I realized that it would take me three years before I could hope to be promoted. This was clearly far too long for me to wait. The normal "career path" at American was not for me.

I was in training for the next two months and then became a ticket agent. The day I started as a ticket agent I also started my own promotion plan. This plan has served me well for my entire business career. In essence, the plan was simple, although in execution it required extra work on a daily basis. The plan was to immediately select the next job I wanted. I then set out to learn to do that job as well as the person currently holding the position. When the job became available, I was known to be more qualified than any of the other candidates.

The results of this strategy quickly became evident. I was promoted in three months rather than three years. I then went on to have seven additional promotions in my next eight years at American Airlines. I left American as a senior director at corporate headquarters to take a position as vice-president of sales for the Thomas Cook division of Midland Bank. I stayed at Cook for five years and was promoted five times until I became executive vice-president and a member of the board of directors. I left Cook in 1979 and started my own investment business in which I buy, start, or sell companies.

I've learned a lot and made my share of mistakes. Some of the maxims that I've learned along the way keep repeating themselves no matter what business or company with which I'm involved. For a number of years, I've been coining my own slogans and collecting others. Many were given to me by numerous business associates and friends. Some of these maxims seemed to have a grain of truth to them at the time, but didn't last over time. A lot of the glib phrases seeking to pass themselves off as truth during the 1980s are clearly laughable now. Those I've consigned to the circular file. What you'll find here are the ones that are keepers: phrases, sayings, and insights that, if applied to your business life, will stand you in good stead for decades. They are not all mine—many if not most were passed on to me by friends and associates. Where possible, I've tracked down the original source. Others have entered into this book as a kind of "folk wisdom"—anonymous axioms that work and keep on working when tested against hard and sometimes painful experience. And so I'd like to acknowledge all the originators of these sayings—known and unknown—and hope that their accumulated wisdom can help my readers along the road to success in business.

They certainly helped me earn thirteen corporate promotions in as many years and go on to earn millions of dollars in my own business ventures.

Why Climb
the Corporate Ladder
When You Can Take
the Elevator?

1

Always be working on your next promotion.

2

Your example is more important than your advice.

3

"Practice does not make perfect. Only perfect practice makes perfect."

—Vince Lombardi,
coach, NFL

4

Anyone in business who burns his bridges better be a damn good swimmer.

5

Unfortunately, in this day and age a verbal contract isn't worth the paper it's written on.

6
Never mistake a slogan for a solution.

7
Most stockbrokers recognize that it's better to live within your means . . . even if you have to borrow money to do it.

8

If you want people to read what you write, master the one-page memo.

Brevity is the soul of promotability in business. In the "information economy," those who use information economically are read and remembered. The higher up in the organization, the less time there is for dealing with organizational minutia. A concept that seems complicated to you will seem overly complex to someone who has to deal with twenty similar concepts in a day. And since it is human nature to deal with the slim-looking issues first, you'd best render the fat out of your memos and reports before you send them up.

9

People who make business decisions with their hearts usually end up with heart disease.

10

Have a wide enough sphere of interests that you don't always talk shop.

11

If you're staff, spend some time on the line. If you're on the line, spend some time with the staff.

12

The proper use of personal notepaper can sometimes be more important than the use of corporate stationery.

13

When you need financing, "No" is not an acceptable answer. It's just your cue to look elsewhere.

14

Know where to get your industry's news and gossip.

15

Your advertising has to be at least as good as your product.

16

Some of the most important people in your company are in the mail room. They know everything.

17

Most consultants first ask corporate executives what advice they are seeking and then later give them that advice.

18

"You miss 100 percent of the shots you never take."

—Wayne Gretzky

19

People who "play office" should go back to kindergarten.

Always ask for the business.

I find it incredible how many salespeople don't ask for the business. They arrive at an appointment and immediately lose sight of their objective—to get a sale. They focus all their attention on "making the presentation." At the end they say, "Why don't you think about it?" Or, "I'll give you a call next week to answer any questions." These statements accomplish nothing.

Instead, a good salesperson should always say, "May I place an order?" If that seems too harsh for you, then try, "What is it going to take to get an order?" The prospect must respond by either buying your product or giving you the reasons for not buying. Answer any objections one by one and, at some point, the prospect will run out of objections and buy the product. It seems simple and it is; but for some mysterious reason, millions of salespeople resist this crucial step.

As this book is being written, I am involved in directing the management of a food company and recently discussed this problem with the company's vice-president of sales. I asked him to strengthen his efforts to "ask for the business." He should end his presentations to the buyer with, "Let's try the product. Do you want two or three pallets to get started?" By saying this, we've made the primary decision: *to ship the product*. The buyer can now make the secondary decision: *how much product?* Our fallback, if the buyer is still not sold, is to say, "We'll ship one pallet, to test it." This is a compromise, but it makes a sale.

21

Any meaningful idea in business is able to be stated in less than one minute.

22

The problem with successful small companies is that as soon as they get big, they usually forget what made them successful.

23

"When you reach for the stars, you may not quite get one, but you won't come up with a handful of mud, either."
—Leo Burnett,
chairman, Leo Burnett Company, Inc.

24

It doesn't matter how many pails of milk you spill, just don't lose the cow.

25

To build a winning business team, hire people who can replace you.

"When you've made your point, shut up and sit down. When you've tried and failed to make your point, shut up and sit down."

—Sol Slotnik, attorney

27

When you've got a good banker, take him to lunch from time to time . . . not just when you need money.

28

The executive on the fast track doesn't wait for tomorrow. Do it now.

29

"Work done with little effort is likely to yield little results."

—B. C. Forbes

30

It is easier to get forgiveness than permission.

31

Unless you enjoy playing Russian roulette with five bullets, never cheat on your expense account.

32

Given a sufficient number of people and an adequate amount of time, one can create insurmountable opposition to most inconsequential ideas.

33

If you think you can, you can. And if you think you can't, you're right.

34

Your desk should be a distribution center, not a warehouse.

Always carry a yellow pad.

The yellow pad is not only a tool for gathering information, it is the ultimate corporate fashion accessory, and much more. The uses of the pad are legion, but some of the top ones are:

1. No matter where you are going or what you are doing, people will believe it is business related.

2. It allows you the right to pass any receptionist without being challenged.

3. It allows you the right to leave the building and go home early without issue.

4. It allows you the right to return from lunch late.

5. It looks more professional than showing up at a meeting without one.

6. It gives the impression that you are more in control.

7. It provides the ability to escape from boring meetings by writing to your mother.

8. It allows you the ability to actually take notes. Besides creating the impression that you are paying attention, the yellow pad helps you actually to do so. Careful notes reduce the inherent ambiguities in receiving instructions.

"I would rather lose in a cause that will someday win, than win in a cause that will someday lose."

—Woodrow Wilson

37

Neatness counts.

38

Praise loudly and criticize quietly.

39

Never treat your subordinates as inferiors.

40

Your memory is made of paper . . . keep great notes.

Be the first in and the last out.

One of my very successful friends who endorsed this book used to, as a junior executive, always buy two suit jackets. He would keep the extra one on the back of his door. When he went home, he always put the extra jacket on the back of his chair.

No matter who went by his office at any time, he was still there even when he wasn't.

Imagine how much *more* successful he would be if he actually was in the office as much as his jacket.

42

Corporate bullies create corporate turnover.

43

If they don't call you back in a week, they probably won't.

44

You can't steal second base if you always keep one foot on first.

45

"When you win, nothing hurts."

—Joe Namath

46

It isn't the people you fire who make your life miserable, it's the ones you don't.

47

"If you can touch it, you can catch it."

—Vince Lombardi,
coach, NFL

48

Revise your five-year plan every six months.

49

"Buy on the rumor. Sell on the news."

—Bernard Baruch

50

"If you shoot, shoot to kill."

—J. Edgar Hoover

51

When you make a mistake, admit it.

52

A career should be a quest not for perfection, but for a high batting average.

53

Don't take calls when in meetings.

54

"Motivation comes from the Significant Principle: Everyone wants what he or she does to be Significant. Make it true and make them believe it."

—Tom Oliver,
executive vice-president,
Federal Express

55

When you find you don't love your job, look for another.

56

If the only tool in your toolbox is a hammer, you tend to treat all opportunities as nails.

57

Never knock the competition. Find out what they are doing right and tell your employees.

58

Better to ask twice than to lose your way once.

59

Never condone racism or sexism or bigotry of any kind.

60

"There's a fine line between being colorful and a real asshole, and I hope I'm still just colorful."

—Ted Turner

61

Leave your business at your office or you'll leave your marriage at your lawyer's.

62

Try to remember all names and faces, not just the "important" ones.

63

"Advice is what we ask for when we already know the answer but wish we didn't."

—Erica Jong

64

Act and look professional and people will think you are.

65

If your company offers educational opportunities, make use of them.

66

Watch your manners. Others are.

67

"Market research has established beyond the shadow of a doubt that the egg is a sad and sorry product and that it obviously will not sell. Because, after all, eggs won't stand up by themselves, they roll too easily, are too easily broken, require special packaging, look alike, are difficult to open, won't stack on the shelf."

—Robert Pliskin,
vice-president, Benton & Bowles

68

Have an interesting life story. If it isn't, work on it, but don't make it an epic.

69

Anyone rude enough to ask your compensation should be given a much higher number.

70

Always remember that you spend at least eight to ten hours of your waking day with your secretary and only three to four hours a day with your wife . . . and that your wife knows it. Send flowers once in a while for no reason at all . . . to your wife.

71

If you covet your boss's job, learn how to do it better than he or she does.

72

Try to take the corner office.

73

Know your receptionist by name . . . or she might forget yours.

74

Join a club that at least one member of your board belongs to.

75

"If you don't do it excellently, don't do it at all. Because if it's not excellent, it won't be profitable or fun, and if you're not in business for fun or profit, what the hell are you doing there?"

—Robert Townsend,
author of *Up the Organization*
and former CEO of Avis

76

Never put plastic plants in your office.

77

Have an office party every year.

78

Send handwritten thank-you notes to every customer at least once a year.

79

Reward employees who have good ideas. It's contagious.

80

Never insult an alligator until after you've crossed the river.

81

Do it right the first time.

82

Jerks lose their tempers.

83

Write memos to yourself on important sub-
jects and file them carefully.

84

Some executives dream of success while others stay awake and achieve it.

You never go wrong doing the right thing.

It was 5:45 P.M. on a chill November day when I left a meeting at the Grand Hyatt Hotel in New York City. My next appointment was a dinner at Le Cirque Restaurant with the chairman of a major investment banking firm.

As I walked out of the hotel it began to rain heavily. There wasn't a taxi in sight and Le Cirque was twenty-three blocks uptown. My triple-A personality dictated I couldn't stand with fifty other people waiting for a cab. I started to walk . . . very fast. As I walked, I kept glancing over my shoulder in the hope that God would send me a taxi.

The midtown traffic was awful. I was actually walking faster than the cars were moving. As I approached Forty-ninth Street a taxi pulled in next to me and a lady (obviously sent from heaven) jumped out. About ten people raced through the rain to grab my cab but I was into the seat in a nanosecond.

As we started up Park Avenue, the driver remarked that he had seen me way back at the Grand Hyatt Hotel. "You looked hassled. Like you were very late for something important," he said as we stopped at the light at Fifty-third Street. "You looked as hassled as that guy over there."

I looked out the window and saw a man walking as fast as I had been. Tired, wet, and cold he was looking over his shoulder. He was obviously late and also asking God to send him a taxi.

I don't know why, because I'd never done such a thing before, but I rolled down my window and said, as we drew up next to this man, "You look like you're in a hurry. Would you like a ride uptown?" In an instant he was in the cab, clearly relieved to be out of the downpour.

We introduced ourselves, but I didn't focus on his name. He mentioned that he worked at the Colgate Company. Since I had several friends working there at the time, I mentioned their names. He said that he knew them. "Great," I said. "What part of the company do you work in?"

"I'm the chairman," he said. Thirty days later Ruben Mark joined the board of my nonprofit organization that provided funding for high-risk inner-city children.

Since that day, I've always gone out of my way to help other people. It makes you feel good, and you never know who you'll meet.

86

Buy stuff from the lobby newsstand.

87

Don't blame others for your errors. If you're responsible, take the hit.

88

Capital is the fuel of business. How far do you think your car would run on credit?

89

When interviewing a new candidate, ask yourself how you'd feel if this person were working for your largest competitor rather than you.

90

Walk around the office at least once a day.

91

Call everyone back.

92

"Incompetence knows no barriers of time or place."

—Laurence J. Peters,
author of *The Peter Principle*

93

Be careful when doing business with people who drive Rolls Royces.

94

If you think something is wrong, it probably is.

95

Hire an assistant who can spell.

96

In the race for success, the speed of the leader determines the pace of the pack.

97

Get a complete physical once a year.

98

Allow an extra two weeks for every deadline.

99

Never have more than two drinks on an airplane unless it's the return flight.

100

Success is a journey, not a destination.

101

Don't allow smoking in your office.

102

Tell your assistant he or she looks great at least once a month.

103

A good driver knows when to put the pedal to the metal and when to hit the brakes.

104

If you get to the boardroom through the bedroom, the honeymoon is usually very short.

105

Ask your boss if he or she has recently lost weight.

106

Take your assistant to lunch, but not too often.

107

Unless you sell aquariums, don't have a tank of fish in your office.

108

"Don't accept your dog's admiration as conclusive evidence that you are wonderful."

—Ann Landers

109
Remember important birthdays.

110
Have a favorite restaurant and make sure the waiters know your name.

111
Beat your boss at golf and he'll want to play more often. If he doesn't, you're as good as fired and it doesn't matter.

112
Avoid shortcuts. They always take too much time in the long run.

113
Look busy. Never wear your suit jacket at work.

114
"You can't score if you keep the bat on your shoulder."

—Casey Stengel

115

Get at least three bids for every job.

116

Don't shoot the messenger. Give him a letter-bomb to take back.

117

In business you cannot discover new oceans unless you have the courage to leave the shore.

118

Demand excellence from every employee . . . including yourself.

119

Drink and corporate drive don't mix.

120

Come to work at 6:00 A.M. and leave at 8:00 P.M. once a month.

121

Remember all who were working at 6:00 A.M. and 8:00 P.M. and give them a raise.

122

If no one is ever at work at 6:00 A.M. or 8:00 P.M., your company is in trouble.

123

Resist giving your bosses advice. Offer suggestions that allow them to reach the same conclusion.

124

"Keep your face to the sunshine and you cannot see a shadow."

—Helen Keller

125

The best consultants find out the facts by interviewing your employees. Why can't you do that?

Never cry.

Fire all regional sales managers whose best customers don't know them by their first name.

"It takes five years of very hard work to become an instant success."

—William A. Shea, Jr.,
Shea & Gould

Analyze the facts before making key decisions.

On June 25, 1876, General George Armstrong Custer received information that a significant number of Indians were gathering at the Little Big Horn. Without analyzing the facts, he decided to ride out with 250 men to "surround" almost 3,000 Indians.

This was a serious mistake.

130

Have a firm handshake.

131

Send your customers "something" in the mail often.

132

Treat your employees as you treat your boss.

133

Never pay for work before it's completed.

134

If you interview someone and don't immediately like him, don't hire him. The odds are that your instincts are right.

135

Don't eat chili before a board meeting.

136

Visit your top fifty customers at least once a year.

Attacks must be answered. An assertion unanswered is an assertion agreed to.

Never miss your fourth putt when playing golf with a good customer.

Know some Yiddish.

If you are going to buy a dead horse, make sure you either know CPR or where to sell the parts.

Build a good Rolodex. Contacts make all the difference.

"Only the fittest will survive, and the fittest will be the ones who understand their office's politics."

—Jean Hollands

Negotiate from strength.

In 1983 I was a principal in a major transaction with a well-known financier. Fortunately this man was on my side, and a major investment banking company was on the other. The final negotiating session was held around a huge circular conference table made of plate glass in the financier's office.

Twelve executives sat around the glass table, which was strewn with papers and stacks of files. It also held a magnificent Steuben glass ashtray weighing at least fifteen pounds.

We were heatedly arguing a final point that was worth about $100,000 in this multimillion-dollar deal. At a crucial moment, my partner stood up, blasted the room with a stream of shouted profanitics, picked up the ashtray and slammed it down into the center of the glass table.

It is hard to express how shocking it was for twelve grown men to be suddenly sitting in a circle no longer occupied by a table. The table had ceased to exist, and shattered glass carpeted the room.

The other side—white with shock—collapsed, conceded the $100,000-deal point, and promptly left the meeting.

As soon as they were out of the room, I asked my partner if he had gone completely insane. He looked at me calmly and said, "That table cost me $10,000. I go through about twelve of them a year. At an average profit of $90,000 per table, I'm more than a million dollars ahead in tables each year."

[Editor's note: When the author's wife read this story, she said, "I remember that guy. I hated him."]

144

Don't ever get drunk at a business lunch.

145

Have your suits cleaned often.

146

If you see something interesting in a magazine or newspaper, tear it out and circulate it to your colleagues and staff.

147

"Rule #1: The customer is always right. Rule #2: If the customer is ever wrong . . . reread Rule #1."

—Stew Leonard

148

Make a Xerox copy of the contents of your wallet before you lose it.

149

Never hire a security guard who wears a bow tie.

150

Call when you are going to be late.

151

Use venture capital only when absolutely necessary.

152

Never compromise your integrity.

153

Encourage your delivery truck drivers to carry dog biscuits in the suburbs.

154

"If a cluttered desk is the sign of a cluttered mind, what is an empty desk a sign of?"

—Eric Klar,
executive vice-president,
Greenfield Healthy Foods

155

Put guest parking spaces nearest the entrance.

156

Sometimes the most impressive or intelligent thing you can say in a meeting is nothing.

157

Never sit with your back to a door.

158

If the meeting is very important, don't fly overseas on a night flight. Take an extra day and go on a day flight.

159

If you are successful in business, don't show up at your kid's school with your driver and limo.

160

Share the credit.

161

Fall behind on deadlines and you'll fall behind in business.

162

Don't delegate office security or fire safety, and never take either for granted.

163

Reconfirm all business meetings—especially if you have to fly to get there.

164

Anytime you must "rush" to make a good business deal . . . pass. Another good deal will always come along.

165

Fix it now . . . or it will still be there tomorrow—only worse.

166

Sue first.

Get paid what you are really worth.

As your time at a corporation stretches from months to years, an interesting thing happens. Management gets to know all your good qualities and also your bad qualities. When a possible promotion for you comes along, management evaluates the "total you" for the position. This includes a recognition of your faults.

If a higher position becomes available at another company and you become a candidate, the management of the new company really doesn't know the "total you." They know only what you tell them and what's written on your resume. Even if they check your references, your references will only highlight your more golden qualities. Because of this, you will always look better and be more promotable to another company.

If you receive a promotion within your present company, you can look for a 10–20 percent increase in compensation along with your new title and responsibilities. If you change companies for a better position, you can earn at least 30 percent more because people pay more to motivate you into leaving a place where you are safe and comfortable. If you have to relocate to a different town, your compensation will be even higher.

In your interview with another company, you should tell them the pay you need to come over to them. Start at a minimum of 40 percent more than you are paid at your present company. You can always trade dollars for "perks" if you are too high: "OK, I'll take less cash—but give me a company car."

Sometimes an interviewer might ask you what your current salary is. It's really none of their business, but if they are nosy enough to ask, you should be smart enough to tell them a salary number that reflects your true value to your corporation, not just your take-home pay.

168

"Executives who take control make their company happen. The other ones get bogged down in a swamp of bureaucracy."

> —J. E. Antonini,
> chairman and CEO,
> K mart Corporation

169

Hire the handicapped.

170

Financing . . . get as much as you can the first time out.

171

Only buy equipment at wholesale that never needs to be fixed.

172

If you are going to lose your job, be sure it's for what you did . . . not for what you didn't do.

173

Be cautious when doing business with men who wear gold chains around their necks.

174

Never contradict your boss at a board meeting.

175

Support your suppliers. Buy their products.

176

Consultants bring confusion to simplicity, and bill you for the service.

177

If you poke a snake it might bite you.

178

When you need to speak directly to a top executive, call his office before 8:30 A.M. or after 5:30 P.M. Chances are he'll pick up the phone himself.

179

"Always remember: a secret is something you tell to one person at a time."

—Dom Rossi,
president, N. W. Ayer

180

No matter what the situation, always act as you think the chairman would act.

181

Insist that your employees focus on how to get it done, rather than on why it can't be done.

182

"There's a better way to do it. Find it."

—Thomas Edison

183

Spend the extra money . . . buy good shoes.

184

A deal that doesn't close right away usually never does.

185

"Don't mistake control for leadership."

—C. Everett Koop, M.D.

186

Get the whole story before making a decision.

187

A good scare is usually worth more than good advice.

188

A promotion always goes to the employee who is slightly better than the rest of the candidates.

189

One of the biggest mistakes you can make in business is to not compliment your employees—often.

190

Ride the truck with your delivery people at least once a year.

191

Always pick up the lunch tab when you go out with your subordinates.

192

Exercise your body . . . it will build up your mind.

193

Better is always better than bigger.

194

Show up unannounced at a field office at least twice a year.

195

Always sit at the head of the table when attending meetings.

196

If someone is rushing you in an unreasonable fashion, tell them, "You can have it right, or you can have it now. You can't have it right now."

197

Keep a spare toilet kit in the office.

198

"Tell me, I forget; show me, I remember; involve me, I understand."
—Ernst Wynder, M.D.,
president, American Health Foundation

199

Wait at least one hour before speaking to someone who has just screwed up.

200

Hire an answering service with real people, and ditch the voice mail.

You can get anyone on the phone if you level the playing field.

Getting an executive who doesn't know you to take your calls is always tough. However, all executives are basically the same as you are. They get up in the morning, get dressed, go to the office, and then do whatever it is they do for a living.

The trick to getting past their secretary is to communicate on the same interest level or status level as the executive you are trying to reach. The president of one company is more likely to take a call from the president of another company than from its sales manager. The sales manager would have a better chance of getting through to another president if his president directed him to make the call and the sales manager mentioned this to the secretary of the executive he is trying to reach.

Interest works the same way. If you know that the president of a company has a particular interest such as stamp collecting and you have a rare stamp to sell, you would probably get through since you are operating on the same interest level.

I once made a completely cold call to the

White House and got the president of the United States to take my call. I had purchased an option on the property next door to one of his homes. As his new neighbor, he took my call. I told him I was interested in selling the option and thought he might like to suggest a friend. As it turned out, he gave me several names and I flipped my option on the property to one of the people on his list for a substantial profit.

202

Teach key employees everything they need to know about your job.

203

Call your switchboard at least once a month and ask for yourself.

204

Consider prospects who say "No" as opportunities.

205

Many executives have a talent for saying the correct thing at the proper time to the wrong people.

206

"Lord, grant that I may always desire more than I can accomplish."

—Michelangelo

207

If it sounds too good to be true, it usually is.

208

Don't be negative. No one likes a rain cloud. People gravitate to the sunshine.

209

When you pay peanuts, you get monkeys.

210

Know when to cut your losses and move on.

211

Happiness is a positive cash flow.

212

Salvage something from all mistakes . . . learn from them.

213

Watch out for the little things, and the big ones will then take care of themselves.

214

Never talk business with your colleagues in elevators, the restroom, or when you're alone in the customer's meeting room.

215

Don't worry about who's right . . . worry about what's right.

216

If you really want to know what's going on in your business, read your customer mail once a month.

217

In business, unfortunately, virtue is not as respectable as money.

218

Unless you have lots of money, don't work for a boss whose wife is in the Junior League.

219

Nothing less than your best is ever good enough.

220

Avoid debt.

221

The only good thing about flying coach is that your luggage is in the claim area by the time you get there.

222

Never lend money to your boss.

223

"Act. Never get caught reacting."
>—John W. Patten,
>president/publisher, *BusinessWeek*

224

Lawyers earn more from problems than solutions.

225

Try not to do business with someone who has nothing to lose.

226

Employ people who are smarter than you.

227

"Corporations pay for performance, not for potential."

—Robert Downey,
Goldman Sachs

228

Be confident. Short your competitor's stock.

229

"It is easier to be nice than nasty—it conserves energy."

—Charlotte Ford

230

Think big . . . act big . . . and big things happen.

231

If you require eight hours' sleep a night, never own more than $10 million in "key man" life insurance.

232

Try not to bring a lawyer to a business meeting.

233

Business is like riding a bicycle. Either you keep up your speed or you fall down.

234

"If the world consists of doers and checkers, I prefer to be a doer."

—Admiral E. R. Zumwalt

235

Only a mediocre executive is always at his best.

236

Arrive early and leave when it's over.

237

Find an accountant who wants to win the Pulitzer Prize for fiction.

238

Only make a great deal if you have no intention of ever doing business with that person again . . . otherwise, make a good deal.

239

Nothing happens until someone sells something.

240

If you have to give business cards to your good customers, you haven't seen them enough.

241

Never admit to anyone that you have re-gripped your golf ball retriever.

242

Always take a call from a headhunter . . . you never know when you'll need him.

243

Any customer dumb enough to ask your profit margin should be given a much lower number.

244

Avoid buying a new piece of equipment for your business unless you know exactly when and how it will pay for itself.

245

Throw out the highest and lowest bids.

246

When naming a new product, always remember that Americans don't like to buy something they can't pronounce.

You get what you pay for.

A popular story within the cruise line industry relates that on April 12, 1912, a British citizen, Mr. Ralph Hendersen, successfully argued that he shouldn't have to pay the full rate for his outside cabin on his cruise ship. Hendersen pointed out that the ship was new and its crew was still learning the various service routines of the ship. Reluctantly, he was given a 10 percent discount by the reservations manager of the H.M.S. *Titanic*.

248

Be sure your handwriting is easily deci-
phered.

249

For every complaint you receive, assume
there are two dozen people who didn't write.

250

Don't lose customers. Working with a new
customer takes 25 percent more effort than
doing the same work with an established customer.

251

If you're not sure whether to do it or not
. . . do it.

252

The reason why worry kills more executives
than hard work is that more executives worry
than work hard.

Be early for meetings.

I once worked for a boss who demanded punctuality at meetings. He installed a lock on the conference room door. If the meeting was scheduled to start at 9:00 A.M. sharp, he would lock the door at precisely 9:00 A.M. and refuse to open it. You only needed to be locked out once to be motivated never to be late again. To this day, I try to be early for all meetings.

254

When you want something done quickly, give it to the busiest person in your office.

255

In business, your most important asset is your reputation.

256

At a party, never dance slow with your boss's spouse.

257

Avoid making decisions your employees can make.

258

Forget hiring a man who parts his hair in the middle.

259

If you don't use the prospect's first name in your presentation, you aren't a great salesperson.

Dig where the gold is . . . unless you just need some exercise.

Always negotiate on a deadline: 90 percent of the agreement will come in the last 10 percent of the time available.

Never allow yourself to be bullied.

Don't even think about responding to call waiting. In fact, ditch it.

Having the newest technology is not always right for business. Call waiting is the perfect example. Call waiting is a telephone service that, I am convinced, was expressly designed to annoy as many people as possible in as short a time as possible. When you are in the middle of an important call with someone who has call waiting, there is a little beep when a second call comes in, and then the following usually happens:

1. He or she will probably cut you off while trying to connect with the other party. The silent message here is that you are not important enough for his or her undivided attention.

2. Assuming you are not cut off while waiting, you completely lose your train of thought, to say nothing of the continuity of your presentation.

3. In the midst of the other call, the person you were speaking with forgets what you were saying.

4. You get a knot in your stomach waiting for the other party to come back on the line.

5. The new caller gets a rude fast shuffle so

the person you were calling can get back to you.

Nobody except the phone company wins from call waiting. On balance, a busy signal is much better. People still know what it means. It means you are busy.

264

You can't be seen if you hide in your office.

265

"I've never been impressed by someone who does eight hours' work in twelve."

—Ralph Giannola,
vice-president of marketing,
Marriott Corporation

266

The longer the title, the less important the person.

267

When checking references, always ask, "Would you hire this person again?" Any answer other than "Yes" is a "No."

268

If your work ends at five, it's a job. If it goes beyond that time, it's a career.

269

Employees who like their jobs will like their customers.

270

Good planning always costs less than good reacting.

271

Support businesses that support education.

272

Lend . . . don't borrow.

273

Never ignore the infrastructure . . . it's what holds everything together.

274

"When considering an investment, remember that the future is longer than the present."

—William A. Shea, Jr.,
Shea & Gould

Don't sell the American public short. They will pay a bit extra for quality.

"People who say, 'Winning isn't everything; it's how you play the game,' should move to Buffalo."

—anonymous NFL coach

"When you step in the gutter, you always get mud on your shoes." Stay away from low-life people and low-life situations.

Always pick up the "cheap" lunch tabs.

"Nothing for nothing is nothing." . . . If you don't put any real effort into something, you can't expect to realize any measurable gains.

280

The harder you work, the luckier you get.

281

If your corporation is one that is dumb enough to be run by a committee, be on that committee.

282

Brainpower in business is more powerful than horsepower.

283

"The road to success is always under construction."

—John W. Patten,
president/publisher, *Business Week*

284

Awards, recognition, and exposure don't pay the bills. The true test of any marketing effort is in the amount of revenue produced.

285

Never go to a meeting unprepared.

286

Be the first to say hello.

287

Make sure someone in the company owns a pickup truck.

288

Be a customer. Call your own switchboard once a quarter and try to buy something.

289

Unless job applicants have also coached Little League, worked in a soup kitchen, helped the Salvation Army, or done some other community service . . . don't hire them.

290

Don't ask a tire salesman if you need new tires.

291

You know it's time to retire when nobody knows the difference.

Treat problems like new opportunities.

In the early 1960s, American Airlines wasn't computerized at its flight departure gates, and used a manual seat-selection system. Obviously, the gate agent would assign window and aisle seats first and the less desirable center seats last. This created a problem with businesspeople who arrived late and hated being crowded between two other passengers.

To solve this problem, I would put a circle around the window or aisle seat assigned to any attractive ladies or men who boarded the plane. When a businessman or businesswoman became irate over a center seat, I would reassign them to a seat next to one of my magnificent passengers and tell them, "Trust me. This will be a great flight. I've seated you next to someone very nice."

This one simple solution to a vexing problem earned me several dozen letters of commendation from passengers.

293

If you're not sure you'll need it long term, rent it.

294

It usually takes as much time to sell a cheap product as it does to sell an expensive one . . . the difference is in the amount of commission earned.

295

Have interesting books in your office.

296

When you accept free tickets, don't complain about the show.

297

Never let what you can't do interfere with what you can do.

298

If you pick up the phone, you own the problem. Deliver the answer.

299

Shoot high.

300

Get what you can and keep what you have and you will someday be rich.

301

Don't try to do something cheaply that shouldn't be done at all.

302

"When the boss lets his hair down too much, he ends up like Rodney Dangerfield. No respect."

—Lee Iacocca

303

When you need to know if you trust a man, ask yourself if you'd play poker with him over the telephone.

304

There is almost nothing in this world that some dumb executive can't make of poorer quality and sell for a cheaper price.

305

Take risks.

306

Don't be foolish and vote for the best president. Vote for the one who will do the least harm.

307

There are two ways to build a successful business: by one's own industry, or by the stupidity of one's competition.

308

No cute messages on your answering machine or voice mail. Ever.

309

On long business trips, ship your luggage via Federal Express.

310

"Some days the dragon wins."

—Peter Rogers,
former chairman, Nabisco Brands

311

Keep a pad and pencil by your bed.

312

No matter where you're going, always carry a business card.

313

Smart executives know when to join a parade in which they have no interest in order to get where they want to go.

314

In business a man should not be judged by what he eats so much as with whom he eats.

315

The wise CEO knows that every great chair-man was once a junior executive.

316

A concerned investment banker is one who blows the horn on his BMW as he drives through a red light.

317

Just because you're often right doesn't mean you're always right.

318

Stupid executives tend to become best friends with other stupid executives.

319

"Throw strikes. Home plate don't move."

—Satchel Paige

All businesspeople can be reduced to two distinct categories: those who borrow, and those who lend.

Inherited wealth has promoted more executives than hard work.

Blessed are those who travel in circles, for they shall be known as wheels.

If all executives thought before they spoke, the silence would be deafening.

Never check anything irreplaceable onto an airplane.

325

All junior executives should know that if they work hard eight hours a day, every day, they could be promoted to senior executive so that they can work hard for twelve hours a day.

326

"There are two times in a man's life when he should not speculate—when he cannot afford it, and when he can."

—Mark Twain

Your best investment is always in people.

In the late 1970s I was involved in several business deals with a fellow from Santa Barbara, California. He was a likable guy, but his luck in business was awful. Although he built up some success, he financed a large business in 1983 and lost $10 million—just about his entire net worth at the time. The result of this loss was terrible on him. He became increasingly depressed and, at the bottom, attempted suicide.

I found out about his situation through a mutual friend. I then called Ray Chambers, another friend who also knew him well. Ray was the founder and chairman of Wesray at the time and agreed to help. Two days later, Ray and I flew to Santa Barbara on Ray's private jet. Ray lent him $150,000 and I lent him $75,000 to get him on his feet and started again.

Over the years, our mutual friend has continued to struggle, trying to regain his fortunes. Neither Ray nor I have ever been paid back in actual cash. Instead, the fellow we helped has introduced me to some wonderful people; since 1983 I've easily earned ten times the amount I lent him, from the contacts I've met.

And I've learned an even more valuable life lesson from this situation. It takes years to build real friendships; and while the asset of that friendship doesn't ever show up on your balance sheets, it can be as real and valuable as furniture, fixtures, plants, and equipment. Probably even more than all of them put together.

328

Always remember that an army of sheep led by a lion will defeat an army of lions led by a sheep.

329

Ability is nothing without opportunity.

330

Some executives are successful because they act successful. Attitude makes a difference.

331

The beginning is half of every action.

332

The world is divided into people who get things done, and people who get the credit.

333

Avoid keeping pictures of yourself around the office.

334

Operating a business with no advertising is like winking at a beautiful woman in the dark . . . you know what you're doing, but nobody else does.

335

Anyone under the age of fifty who hands you a business card with the word *consultant* on it was probably fired from his last job.

336

If you stay in the middle of the road, the chances of your being run over are doubled.

337

Dumb executives are the ones who expend energy to raise their voice rather than to reinforce their argument.

338

The large print giveth and the small print taketh away.

339

If you want it tomorrow, ask for it yesterday.

340

A free lunch is only found in mousetraps.

341

Absence doesn't make the heart grow fonder in business. Speak to your customers often.

342

Act like a jerk and people will think that you are.

343

People who say winning isn't everything never win.

344

Never use push when you've got pull.

345

"It is not the employer who pays the wages. Employers only handle the money. It's the customer who pays the wages."

—Henry Ford

346

Don't put your name on the first parking space.

347

The wise public-relations executive is a person who thinks twice before saying nothing.

348

Be careful when you stand up to be counted. Someone might take your seat.

349

"If two men on the same job agree all the time, then one is useless. If they disagree all the time, then both are useless."

—Darryl F. Zanuck

350

Lose weight.

351

On Wall Street, ethics is defined as a set of rules created by executives to identify how they would act if their business were profitable.

352

Special interests are called "special" because they have no interest in the general interest.

353

Experience is what you get when you don't get what you want.

354

If you can't break 100, don't play golf with your boss.

355

Fear of becoming a failure keeps most executives from becoming anything.

356

Loyalty bought with money can always be overcome with money.

357

We can't all be executives. Someone has to actually do the work.

358

"The higher you climb the flagpole, the more people see your rear end."

—Don Meredith

359

Executives who make themselves into sheep will probably be eaten by wolves.

360

Foolish ideas dressed up to look impressive are usually dreamed up by impressive fools.

361

"Eighty percent of success is showing up."

—Woody Allen

"Pressure is when you've got thirty-five bucks riding on a four-foot putt and you've only got five dollars."

—Lee Trevino

If everything in business were fair, the losing lawyer wouldn't get paid.

Executives who take cold showers in the morning start the day much more alert. They are also incredible jerks.

Corporate treasurers who can always balance the accounts are usually considered geniuses. Chances are these geniuses are also crooks.

A chain is only as strong as its weakest link.

I realize that this is one of the oldest maxims in the known universe. But in the environment of business and corporate life that depends so much on teamwork, it bears repeating.

When I ran training seminars for new employees at American Airlines, I kept on returning to this old saw. I'd explain to the agents in my group that every day thousands of employees worked incredibly hard to ensure a passenger's loyalty to American Airlines. But if a reservation was wrong, *or* the ticket was written incorrectly, *or* the flight got out late, *or* the crew wasn't friendly, *or* the bag was missing, it didn't matter to the passenger that everything else was perfect. One mistake by one employee could mean that the work of thousands—from the corporate office to the maintenance hangars to the cockpit crew—had gone for naught.

367

Any company with more chiefs than Indians shall be 110 percent ahead of its competition in meetings.

368

"Strive for businesses that complement each other . . . like the man who was a veterinarian and a taxidermist: 'Either way, you get your dog back.' "

—Mike Buckman,
general manager,
American Express

369

Most executives in the 1980s lived so far beyond their incomes that they were forced to purchase BMWs just to catch up.

370

Before borrowing money from a friend, decide which you need most.

Never let personal setbacks distract you from your business.

In 1981 I hired a painter to repaint the front of our brownstone. One morning I rode up onto the scaffold with him to look at the work. When we reached the fourth floor, the scaffold broke. I dropped four stories and landed on an iron fence below. I was rushed to Bellevue Hospital in critical condition.

The doctors told my wife that since I was in great shape I had a good chance of survival. I had been training for my third New York City marathon. Every day for months I had run fifteen miles and was probably in the best condition anyone falling four stories would want to be in.

Although there is never a good time for this sort of thing, it could not have happened at a worse time for my business. I was in the final days of launching a trade show at the New York Coliseum. I had a fortune invested in this business, and each day that I was not selling booth space in the show put the entire venture at risk.

It was this motivation that forced me to get out of the hospital bed two days after the fall, so I could make phone calls to prospects from the pay phone in the hallway at Bellevue. My doctors and my wife went crazy, but, over their objections, I continued to work.

On the fourth day after the fall, the doctors told my wife to take me home. They felt that I was better off working at home than from a cart that I had set up in the hallway at their hospital.

Less than a week after falling from the roof of my building, I returned to the office. Not one of my staff of six could look at me. I looked awful and felt worse, but I saved my business.

No matter what the circumstances, dress for success.

Insanity is grounds for dismissal in most corporations, but is mandatory for success as a stockbroker.

The executive who works from 7:00 A.M. to 7:00 P.M. every day will be both very successful and fondly remembered by his widow's next husband.

Show me an executive who hasn't fantasized about getting in his car and quitting his job, and I'll show you an executive who doesn't drive.

The executive who kisses asses will ultimately be kissed off.

The most valuable lesson one can learn from going to meetings is that most of them are not necessary.

In the 1980s, most bankers were so addicted to exaggeration that they couldn't tell the truth without lying.

Anyone can pilot a ship in a calm sea.

Corporate life is not fair, but you should be.

Most CFOs know that if your outgo exceeds your income, your upkeep will be your downfall.

"Success is more a function of consistent common sense than it is of genius."

—An Wang,
founder of Wang Computer

Some executives create more enthusiasm when they leave a room than when they enter it.

Many corporations encourage independent thinking right up until the day they fire you for it.

The 1980s demonstrated that inaccuracy was not permitted in the corporate world, but lying was totally acceptable.

When a consultant tells you that his fee is "only" $50,000 up front, offer $60,000 but stipulate you'll pay when the job is finished.

A close friend in the consulting business once told me that the justification of fees was one of the most difficult aspects of his job. The more senior the consultant, the greater his or her contacts and the easier it is to get the job done. But if the job looks too easy, the client resists paying a large fee. When confronted with resistance, my friend always tells his clients the following tale:

In 1970, NASA had four astronauts circling the moon. Suddenly, the entire communications center went down and Houston Control could not communicate with the astronauts. NASA technicians couldn't locate the problem, and the mission director was in near panic. In desperation, he called in a well-known communications consultant to help.

This small, slightly built consultant arrived complete with tiny bow tie, horn-rimmed glasses, and a small electronic tool kit belted around his waist. He circled the control center slowly three times, studying the computer and its relays. Finally, he stopped in front of a small relay, reached into his pocket and took out a small rubber mallet. He carefully tapped one particular relay and the entire communications center came back on line instantly. The director was elated.

A week later the director received a bill for $50,000 from the consultant. Irate, the director called the consultant and demanded an explanation for such a charge for tapping a relay with a rubber mallet. The consultant said, "Oh, you've misunderstood my bill. I charged you $1,000 for tapping the relay and $49,000 for knowing where to tap."

387

Even if your entire board of directors votes for a dumb idea, it is still a dumb idea.

388

Not everyone can be a hero. Someone has to sit on the curb and clap as the hero marches by.

389

Management seminars are designed to teach executives new ways to make it difficult for people to get any work done.

390

Any executives who look good, sound good, and act good will get by in corporate life . . . even if they're stupid.

391

Always make sure you have what you need before you begin.

392

Your boss will seldom remember when you are right and never forget when you are wrong.

393

People in meetings tend to agree on decisions that, as individuals, they know are stupid.

394

"Watch all your competitors regardless of size. A small business can become a big problem overnight."

—a former IBM executive

395

Senior executives fall into three categories: those who make things happen; those who watch things happen; and those who wonder what happened.

396

Always sell stock to pessimists . . . they never expect it to go up.

397

Profit is its own reward.

398

Only stupid lawyers would actually solve the problem and eliminate your need to keep paying them. Does that mean you should only hire stupid lawyers if you want to get something done?

399

"Treat success like a lover. It is better to be adventurous than cautious."

—Machiavelli

400

"Nothing will ever be attempted, if all possible objections must be overcome."

—Dr. Johnson

401

Even the greatest skaters sometimes fall through the ice.

402

Any problem that can be solved with a check isn't a problem, it's an expense.

403

Those who have some money think that the most important thing in the world is love. The poor know it's money.

404

Procrastination is the art of keeping up with yesterday.

405

The best job for an employee who constantly says, "Because that's the way we've always done it," is with one of your competitors.

When you make every sale a good buy for your customer, that customer will become a good customer.

If you wait for an opportunity to emerge, all your competitors will be there to help you take advantage of it. If you can find opportunities before they emerge, your competitors will be forced to follow you.

"One must never be satisfied doing only what one can; one must always do what one really cannot."

—Niels Bohr

Keep a dictating machine in your car.

A good salesperson can sell a bridge where there is no water.

411

An unreasonable price when buying becomes quite reasonable when selling.

412

If you are making a commission, say so up front.

413

All criticism should be constructive.

414

If you think you can get something for nothing in business, you shouldn't be in business.

415

Never delegate responsibility without authority.

416

Spread authority over many people and decisions will be made much more efficiently.

If your only choice is to hire either an obnoxious executive or a foolish executive, hire the obnoxious one—occasionally he won't be obnoxious.

Ask questions.

The average customer who has been pleased by a company tells three people about it. The average customer who has had a problem with a company tells ten people about it.

A lean compromise is better than a fat lawsuit.

Share your success and you will be more likely to repeat it.

A round peg will never fit into a square hole. Get the right employee for the right job, or you'll have an unhappy employee and a botched job.

Be cautious when doing business with men who wear diamond pinkie rings.

"I made a fortune getting out too soon."

—J. P. Morgan

No single job has a future. Only you have a future.

"It's not just whether it's legal or illegal; it's whether it's right or wrong."

—Ralph Giannola,
vice-president of marketing,
Marriott Corporation

427

Know when to hold.
Know when to fold.

428

A good salesperson can drop a feather into the Grand Canyon and have you standing there waiting for the echo.

429

When you meet a businessperson who tells you it isn't the money but the principle, you've met either a fool or a liar.

430

In business, as in sailing, it is easier to adjust the sails than to try to direct the wind.

431

In whatever you say to a customer, consistency is the key. Therefore it is both easier and wiser to be truthful.

432

Never assume that the customer can't afford what you are offering.

433

The best way to convince a foolish executive he is wrong is to let him have his way.

434

Seek and publicize testimonials.

435

Always start out by asking for more than you really need.

436

As a person in business, if you have intelligence you don't need to have much else; if you don't have intelligence, it doesn't matter what else you have.

437

Obligations are bankable.

438

Lead, follow, or get out of the way.

439

Learn to recognize when people are not listening to you.

440

The more you need your job, the worse you will be treated.

441

Anyone who thinks he or she is indispensable should stick a finger in a bowl of water and notice how long the hole stays there after the finger is pulled out.

442

No one ever drowned in their own sweat.

443

Build strong alliances.

444

The carrot is a hundred times more effective than the stick, and you don't have to worry about being hit back.

445

On making it to the summit, your first move should be to turn around and offer a hand up to the person behind you.

446

The best time to sell a horse is before it dies.

447

Strive to be constantly consistent.

448

Never act out of malice.

449

Don't let group-think keep you from expressing your honest thoughts and feelings.

450

Half-finished work is labor lost.

451

Always be learning.

452

If you are ill at ease when speaking, practice.
If you are comfortable speaking, practice.

453

In a speech, make each point three times.

If you wish to succeed . . . maintain a positive attitude.

In business, as in life, every issue, decision, or opportunity contains both a positive and negative aspect. All too often in the corporate world, many executives focus on why something won't work rather than on the ways in which something will work. After hours of discussion, negatively focused executives will have arrived at the best reason not to do something. These types tend to be known as the Abominable No-Men. Had they spent the same time focused on how to make something happen, they may well have created a new product or service that would provide greater revenue to their company.

I recently funded the launch of a start-up company called Greenfield Healthy Foods that makes wholesome, great-tasting snacks. Once I saw how much consumers loved these snacks, I set out to raise several million dollars in additional capital. This was at the beginning of the 1990s, probably the worst time to try to raise money since the Great Depression. But I was positive that the company's concept was correct. I wanted to sell 30 percent of the company. Over one hundred investors turned me down, but sixteen didn't, and I raised all of the capital required.

By the company's third year, its sales were going straight up and the value of Greenfield Healthy Foods was $20 million and climbing.

Clearly Greenfield would never have been started—much less have become successful—had everyone involved not had very positive attitudes. In these difficult economic times, it is essential for all chief executives to maintain positive attitudes if they want their companies to grow. A negative perspective limits self-confidence and the ability to take necessary risks. If you focus hard enough on why something won't work, chances are it won't.

455

An idea can turn to dust or magic, depending on the talent you rub it with.

456

There's no such thing as a hard sell or a soft sell. There's only the stupid sell and the smart sell.

457

Worry about the careers of those who work for you and then yours will thrive.

458

Keep to both the letter and the spirit of your agreements.

459

If you don't drive your business, you'll be driven out of business.

460

Suggest solutions when you present problems and you'll pave the way to your own promotion.

461

A clean desk means someone else is doing all the work.

462

In business, the only disease worse than alcoholism is egotism.

463

Trade associations have no heads. They have only necks that have grown hair on top.

464

The only really good sale is made when the customer gets a good buy.

Sometimes it is better to retreat.

Napoleon, like many foolish generals before and after him, thought it would be a good idea to invade Russia in 1812. He set out from Poland in the spring with 450,000 men and advanced toward Moscow. The Russians, faced with overwhelming force, retreated before Napoleon—being careful to burn everything behind them. By September, Napoleon was on the outskirts of Moscow and was finally engaged in battle at Borodino. The outcome of that battle was inconclusive, and Napoleon came on toward Moscow.

Forced to choose between saving Moscow and saving the Russian army, General Kutuzov chose to save the army and abandoned Moscow to the French, retreating still farther into Russia. Napoleon took Moscow but knew that he could not hold it through the winter.

Unlike the Russians who had *chosen* to retreat, Napoleon was *forced* to retreat. An army that numbered 450,000 when it began its advance on the retreating Russians emerged from Russia that winter with fewer than 10,000 troops. The Russians had long since moved back into Moscow.

466

If you want to communicate effectively, be careful you don't say too much.

467

To get where you want to go, you sometimes have to go in the opposite direction.

468

Using only market research to make decisions is like driving a car using a rearview mirror.

469

Common sense and consistency will succeed more frequently than raw genius.

470

Once solved, all problems are simple.

471

"Always swing hard, in case you happen to hit the ball."

—Duke Snider

472

One manager from the factory is worth ten
from law school.

473

Don't tell employees how to do the job . . .
tell them what needs to be done.

474

The history of business teaches us that, as
bad as things are now, they will be "the good
old days" ten years from now.

475

Management recruiters like to offer good
jobs to people who already have good jobs.

476

When traveling abroad it is best to remember that money, not English, is the international language.

477

Brilliant ideas are those that were first thought to be wrong but later shown to be obvious.

478

If you know how, you'll always have a job. If you know why, you'll be the boss.

479

"A little humility makes you perfect."

—Ted Turner

480

Eat in the company cafeteria at least once a week.

481

If you never made a mistake, you never made anything.

482

When your ideas meet with silence, don't assume consent. People may just not be listening.

483

To succeed, be daring, be first, be different.

484

Don't be afraid that your computers will start to think like you . . . be afraid that you will start to think like your computers.

485

Leadership is action, not position.

486

The ability to recognize ability is a very rare ability.

487

Products need people to survive.

488

A business traveler knows that his office has booked him into the wrong hotel when the chalk outline on the floor overlaps with a second one.

489

Attitude is a little thing that makes a big difference.

490

The first thing that happens when you become chairperson is that all your acquaintances from high school whom you haven't heard from for thirty years remember that they were your best friend.

491

Don't wear your best suit to a union negotiation.

492

If you realize that you've just said something stupid, immediately attribute it to your competition.

493

If the hardest part of the job is finding a parking place, your employees may start parking in your biggest competitor's lot.

Keep current. Read a newspaper every day.

One morning I read in the *New York Times* business section that a subsidiary of a major corporation had posted a loss that could only be described as fatal. I thought, "If I were the chief financial officer of the parent corporation, I'd like to sell this division in the worst way." I picked up the phone and made a cold call to the CFO. I got his assistant on the phone and told her I had a client interested in buying the ailing division. It took only seconds for the CFO to be on the line inviting me to stop by and see him at the earliest opportunity. I went over that afternoon and met the CFO. Sure enough, he was more than ready to sell the division. When he asked me who my client was, I told him that I wasn't in a position to divulge that information at that time.

I left his office with all the necessary financials and went directly to the public library. I made a list of every company in the same business category that might be in the market to expand. I started cold-calling the president of each company. I told each assistant that I was calling to see if the president might be interested in the purchase of a competing company. Every president took my call. On the eighth call I found a company in the expansion mode. Sixty days later the deal was done and I earned a $200,000 finder's fee. To me this was living proof that you can get your job through *The New York Times.*

495

The primary use of airline timetables is to identify just how late the plane is.

496

If you make your employees feel bad, they'll wind up only doing the things that they think will make you feel good.

497

Accept the fact that half your advertising dollar will be wasted and you will never know which half.

498

On Wall Street it is widely believed that religion was invented to keep the poor from killing the rich.

499

The clergy have it right: cash up front for unlimited real estate in heaven.

500

The difference between an experienced businessman and an educated businessman is that an educated businessman recognizes his mistakes and then makes them again.

ACKNOWLEDGMENTS

I have been creating or collecting business maxims for at least fifteen years as a hobby. I certainly wish to thank Tom Sawyer, Vince Lombardi, and the hundreds of others who originally created so much of the wisdom I have included in this book.

I especially wish to thank Gerard Van der Leun, my agent and partner, for his insight and creative talent in organizing my collection of thousands of maxims and helping me boil them down to the five hundred that communicate my personal philosophy for business success.

Equally important, this book would not have been possible without the intelligence and vision of Diane Reverand, my publisher at Villard, who recognized that businesspeople everywhere would benefit from much of what I have collected.

Most of all I am grateful to my wife, LaDonna, for her endless love and patience over the past twenty-three years with my constant entrepreneurial endeavors.

Lastly, I wish to thank my mom and dad, for giving me the love, support, and value systems that have helped me achieve success in my personal and business life. While my dad isn't with us any longer, I do believe he knows I have followed his advice.

ABOUT THE AUTHOR

JOHN M. CAPOZZI has held senior corporate management positions for over twenty years. He joined American Airlines in 1966 and, after receiving eight promotions in as many years, left American as a senior director on the corporate marketing staff to become vice-president of sales for the Thomas Cook Travel division of Midland Bank. In his four and a half years at Thomas Cook, Inc., he was promoted four times, was a member of the board of directors of both the Travel Company and the Traveler's Cheque Company, and was responsible for the development of almost $300 million in new business in his first year alone. Mr. Capozzi left Thomas Cook, Inc., in 1979 to devote himself full-time to the development of a marketing, consulting, and investment banking firm. He lives in Connecticut with his wife and two children.

John H. Dasburg,
president & CEO,
Northwest Airlines
"Capozzi has just about covered the corporate waterfront."

William A. Shea, Jr.,
Shea & Gould
"Anyone interested in communicating in the business world must read this book."

Admiral E. R. Zumwalt, Jr.,
U.S. Navy (Ret.)
"This book of collected wisdom in the form of maxims is an enjoyable read for all those of us who seek additional kernels to add to our own wisdom."

Doug John, president,
Connecticut Marketing
Associates
"Can you imagine how great being in business would be if everyone lived their lives according to Capozzi's book?"

Zelig Chinitz,
executive vice-chairman,
World Zionist Organization
"This book constitutes a credo not only for business, but for everyday living."

Edward L. Steinberg, M.Sc.,
O.D., director and chairman,
Slim-Fast International
"Capozzi has collected an arsenal of business bullets that when aimed correctly will surely help the motivated businessman achieve financial success and personal satisfaction."